D1128732

RICHMOND HILL
PUBLIC LIBRARY

JUN 2 2006

RICHMOND GREEN
905-780-0711

BOOK SOLD
NO LONGER R.H.P.L.
PROPERTY

Farmers
Community Workers

by Alice K. Flanagan

Content Adviser: MeeCee Baker, Ph.D., Adjunct Professor,
Department of Agricultural and Extension Education,
North Carolina State University

Reading Adviser: Dr. Linda D. Labbo,
College of Education, Department of Reading Education,
The University of Georgia

COMPASS POINT BOOKS

Minneapolis, Minnesota

Compass Point Books
3722 West 50th Street, #115
Minneapolis, MN 55410

Visit Compass Point Books on the Internet at *www.compasspointbooks.com* or e-mail your request to *custserv@compasspointbooks.com*

Photographs ©: Tom McCarthy/Unicorn Stock Photos, cover; Elliot Smith/ImageState, 4; U.S. Department of Agriculture, 5, 14, 19; Inga Spence/Visuals Unlimited, 6, 23; Michael S. Lewis/Corbis, 7, 22; Inga Spence/Tom Stack & Associates, 8, 25; Deere & Company, 9, 20; Digital Stock, 10; Jeff Greenberg/Visuals Unlimited, 11, 27; Bob Rowan, Progressive Image/Corbis, 12; Annie Griffiths Belt/Corbis, 13; Tim Wright/Corbis, 15; Patti McConville/The Image Finders, 16; Photo Network/Patti McConville, 17; Eric R. Berndt/The Image Finders, 18, 26; Index Stock/Ed Lallo, 21; Photo Network/Gay Bumgarner, 24.

Editors: E. Russell Primm, Emily J. Dolbear, and Pam Rosenberg
Photo Researcher: Svetlana Zhurkina
Photo Selector: Linda S. Koutris
Designer: Bradfordesign, Inc.

Library of Congress Cataloging-in-Publication Data

Flanagan, Alice K.
    Farmers / by Alice K. Flanagan.
        p. cm. — (Community workers)
    Summary: Briefly describes the different kinds of farmers, the food that they grow, the conditions under which they work, their tools and equipment, their problems, and the help they provide to their communities.
    Includes bibliographical references (p.   ).
    ISBN 0-7565-0305-1 (hardcover)
        1. Farmers—Juvenile literature. 2. Agriculture—Juvenile literature. [1. Farmers. 2. Occupations.]
I. Title. II. Series.
    S519 .F544 2002
    630'.92—dc21   2002005165

© 2003 by Compass Point Books
All rights reserved. No part of this book may be reproduced without written permission from the publisher. The publisher takes no responsibility for the use of any of the materials or methods described in this book, nor for the products thereof.
Printed in the United States of America.

Table of Contents

What Do Farmers Do? 5

What Tools and Equipment Do They Use? 7

How Do Farmers Help? 11

Where Do Farmers Work? 13

With Whom Do Farmers Work? 15

What Do Farmers Wear? 17

What Training Does It Take? 19

What Skills Do Farmers Need? 21

What Problems Do Farmers Face? 23

Would You Like to Be a Farmer? 25

A Farmer's Tools and Clothes 26

On the Farm 27

A Farmer's Day 28

Glossary 29

Did You Know? 30

Want to Know More? 31

Index 32

RICHMOND HILL
PUBLIC LIBRARY

JUN 2 2006

RICHMOND GREEN
905-780-0711

What Do Farmers Do?

Farmers grow plants and raise animals. Farmers who grow plants to feed people are called **crop** farmers. Farmers who raise animals for meat, wool, or fur are called **livestock** farmers. **Dairy** farmers raise cows for their milk. **Poultry** farmers raise chickens, turkeys, and other birds for their eggs or their meat.

◀ A Zuni Indian examines his corn crop.

A dairy farmer feeds his livestock. ▶

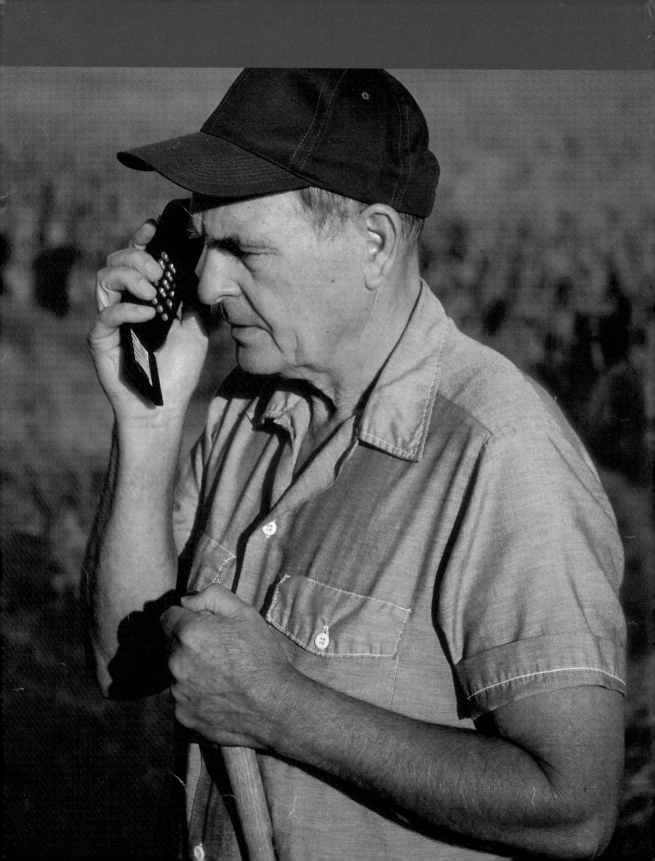

What Tools and Equipment Do They Use?

Farmers use many kinds of tools and equipment. They use shovels to clean out the barn. They use **pitchforks** to lift and throw hay. Farmers might use a cell phone to talk to a worker in the fields. Farmers also use computers to keep a record of what they buy and sell.

◀ A cell phone can come in handy in the fields.

In the winter, a farmer uses a pitchfork to lift hay for his cattle and horses to eat. ▶

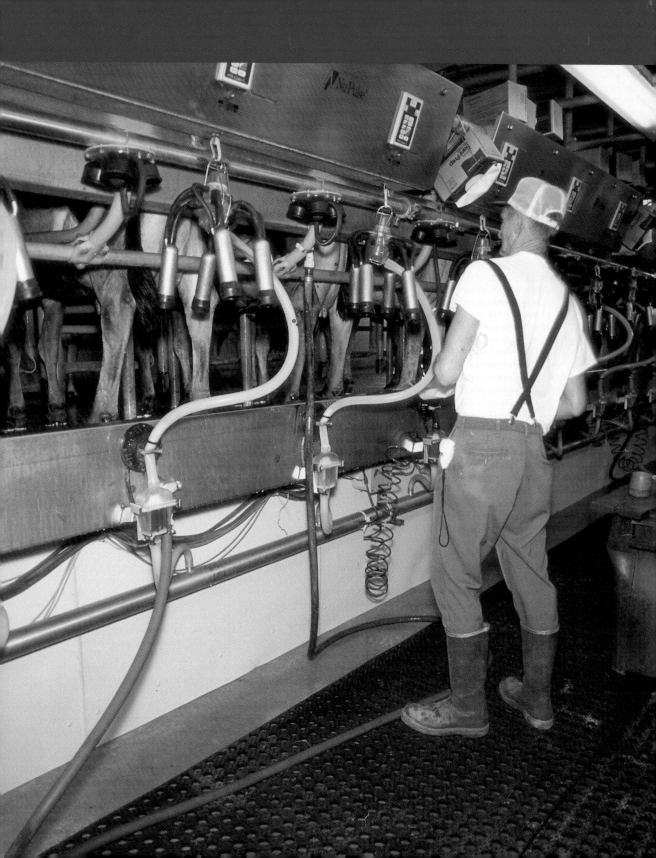

A farmer needs many machines. Dairy farmers use machines to milk the cows. Crop farmers drive tractors to break up the soil, plant seeds, and gather crops. Trucks carry a farm's crops and animals to market. Many farm machines are big and some are very expensive!

Milking machines milk many cows at once.

These farming machines gather wheat crops.

How Do Farmers Help?

Farmers grow and raise much of the food we eat. Without food, we could not live. Farmers raise sheep to get wool for sweaters, rugs, and blankets. Farmers grow cotton plants, too. Did you know that some kinds of tea bags are made of cotton? We need farmers for many items we use every day.

◀ Workers pick heads of lettuce for market.

We need farmers to ▶ supply the food at the market.

Where Do Farmers Work?

Farmers work outdoors in all kinds of weather. They also work in barns that hold animals and equipment. Sometimes they work in **silos**, where grains may be stored. Most farmers also work in their houses. They have a home office where they take care of farm business.

◀ A farmer works in his home office.

A farmer works in the fields. ▶

With Whom Do Farmers Work?

Many farmers work alongside family members. Some hire farm laborers to help them. Everyone on a farm works as a team. **Veterinarians** help farmers keep the animals healthy. Government workers help farmers borrow money for the equipment they need. The government also helps farmers protect the farm's land and water.

Farm managers examine crops together.

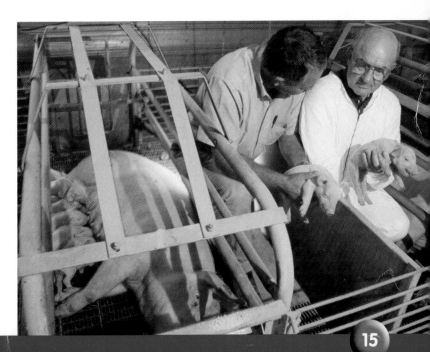

A veterinarian looks at a young pig at a North Carolina farm.

What Do Farmers Wear?

Most farmers wear blue jeans and a shirt or coveralls. They need strong shoes or boots for working in fields and with animals. Work gloves protect their hands. Hats help keep farmers from getting sunburned. In cold weather, farmers wear more layers of clothes to keep warm.

◄ A farmer wears coveralls, boots, gloves, and a cap.

A hat protects this farmer from the sun's rays. ►

What Training Does It Take?

Many future farmers go to college. In college they study several subjects. Science and math classes are useful. They usually get degrees in **agriculture**. **Accounting** classes also help. Students may learn the best plants to grow in each kind of soil. They can also learn how to keep animals and crops healthy.

◄ An agriculture student studies a test wheat crop in Kansas.

An agriculture ► professor teaches his students in the classroom.

What Skills Do Farmers Need?

Farmers need a lot of energy because they work long hours. Running a farm takes planning as well as hard work. Farmers must be good at using—and fixing—farm machines. Farmers need to be quick learners. They must learn the latest information about pests, the soil, and the **climate**.

A young worker fixes farming equipment.

A cattle farmer ▶ tracks his farm's output on a computer.

What Problems Do Farmers Face?

Bad weather can keep a farmer from planting seeds. Machines may break down. Sometimes animals die of disease. Often, insects eat the crops. All of these problems make caring for plants and animals a full-time job. If farmers go on vacation or get sick, they must get someone to take care of their farms.

In Colorado, rain keeps farmers from gathering crops.

Insects can ruin farm plants.

Would You Like to Be a Farmer?

Do you like to grow things? Do you like to raise animals? Do you enjoy working outside? Maybe you would like to be a farmer someday. You can prepare now. In school, learn about soil, weather, plants, and animals. At home, plant a garden and take care of it. Join a club like the 4-H program or the FFA.

◀ A young boy helps care for a garden at home.

Taking part in a 4-H fair can be fun. ▶

A Farmer's Tools and Clothes

tractor

cap

sunglasses

blue jeans

boots

On the Farm

silo

barn

feeding trough

truck

holding pen

fence

farmer

A Farmer's Day

Morning
- The farmer gets up before sunrise. The cattle need water.
- Then he goes to the barn to fix the tractor that broke down yesterday.
- It's breakfast time. The farmer goes back to the house to eat with his family.
- After breakfast, he finishes fixing the tractor in the barn.

Noon
- The farmer eats lunch at his house.
- After lunch, the farmer goes to his home office. He checks on cattle prices and orders some supplies.

Afternoon
- The farmer calls the veterinarian about a pregnant cow that hasn't been eating.
- Now it is time to check on the other cattle.
- It is getting late. The farmer goes back to the house and takes a shower before dinner.

Evening
- The farmer and his family eat dinner together. They discuss the chores each person will do that weekend.
- After dinner, the farmer watches the weather forecast on television.
- Next the farmer goes to check on the herd and pump water.
- Now it is time for bed. Tomorrow, the farmer has to plow the wheat field.

Glossary

accounting—keeping a record of the money a business spends and earns

agriculture—farming

climate—the usual weather expected in a certain place

crop—plants, such as potatoes or wheat, grown in large amounts for food

dairy—a farm where animals, usually cows, are raised for their milk

livestock—animals raised on a farm, such as cows, sheep, pigs, or horses

pitchforks—large forks with long handles and two or three prongs, used for lifting and throwing hay

poultry—birds raised on farms for their eggs or meat

silos—tall towers used to store grain

veterinarians—doctors who take care of animals

Did You Know?

- President Abraham Lincoln founded the U.S. Department of Agriculture in 1862. He called it the "people's department."

- There are more than 2 million farms in the United States.

- Idaho, Iowa, Kansas, Montana, Nebraska, North Dakota, Oklahoma, South Dakota, and Wyoming have more cattle than people.

- Some crayons are made from soybeans. About 1 acre (0.4 hectare) of soybeans can produce 82,368 crayons.

- The average dairy cow gives about 100 half-pint (quarter-liter) school-sized cartons of milk a day.

- Beekeepers raise bees for honey. They also rent their bees to other farmers to help carry pollen to crops.

Want to Know More?

At the Library

Hughes, Sarah. *My Dad Works on a Farm.* Danbury, Conn.: Children's Press, 2001.

Kalman, Bobbie. *Hooray for Dairy Farming!* New York: Crabtree Publishing, 1997.

Rendon, Marcie R., and Cheryl Walsh Bellville (photographer). *Farmer's Market: Families Working Together.* Minneapolis, Minn.: Carolrhoda Books, 2001.

On the Web

From Native Prairie to Present, Our Agricultural Heritage

http://www.campsilos.org

For the history of farming and the many uses for corn

USDA for Kids

http://www.usda.gov/news/usdakids/index.html

For more information about agriculture and the food we eat

Through the Mail

The National 4-H Council

7100 Connecticut Avenue

Chevy Chase, MD 20815

To write for information about 4-H Club programs

On the Road

The Farmers' Museum

Lake Road

Cooperstown, NY 13326

To take part in activities that teach about nineteenth-century farm life and objects

Index

agriculture degrees, 19
barns, 7, 27
cell phones, 7
clothes, 17, 26
computers, 7
crop farmers, 4, 9
dairy farmers, 4, 9
education, 19
farm laborers, 15
food, 5, 11
4-H program, 25
FFA, 25
government workers, 15

home offices, 13
insects, 23
livestock farmers, 4, 11, 23
milking machines, 9
pitchforks, 7
poultry farmers, 4
shovels, 7
silos, 13, 27
tools, 7, 9, 21, 23, 26, 27
tractors, 9, 26
trucks, 9, 27
veterinarians, 15
weather, 13, 21, 23, 25

About the Author
Alice K. Flanagan writes books for children and teachers. She has
written more than seventy books on a wide variety of topics. Some of
her books include biographies of U.S. presidents and their wives,
biographies of people working in our neighborhoods, phonics books
for beginning readers, and informational books about birds and
Native Americans. Alice K. Flanagan lives in Chicago, Illinois.